Rookie
Read-About® Science

Taking Root

WITHDRAWN

By Allan Fowler

Consultants
Linda Cornwell, Coordinator of School Quality
and Professional Improvement
Indiana State Teachers Association

Jan Jenner, Ph.D.

CP Children's Press®
A Division of Grolier Publishing
New York   London   Hong Kong   Sydney
Danbury, Connecticut

Visit Children's Press® on the Internet at:
http://publishing.grolier.com

Designer: Herman Adler Design Group
Photo Researcher: Caroline Anderson
The photo on the cover shows carrots, radishes, and other roots that we eat.

Library of Congress Cataloging-in-Publication Data

Fowler, Allan.
    Taking root / by Allan Fowler.
      p. cm. — (Rookie read-about science)
    Includes index.
    Summary: Describes what roots look like and how they function in plants.
    ISBN 0-516-21591-4 (lib. bdg.)   0-516-27058-3 (pbk.)
    1. Roots (Botany)—Juvenile literature. [1. Roots (Botany).]
  I. Title. II. Series.
  QK644.F686   2000   98-52945
  581.4'98—dc21   CIP
                                            AC

GROLIER
P U B L I S H I N G   1 2 3 4 5 6 7 8 9 10 R 09 08 07 06 05 04 03 02 01 00

Did you know that this boy is eating a root?

4

That's right. The orange part of a carrot plant is its root.

The roots of most plants grow underground. They hold the plants in place.

The roots that hold these tall trees in place grow deep under the ground.

7

The roots of this plant hold the soil in place.

Plant roots help hold
soil together.

When the ground is
not covered with plants,
heavy rains can wash the
soil away.

A root is covered with many tiny hairs.

These hairs take in water and minerals from the soil.

This is how a plant drinks and eats.

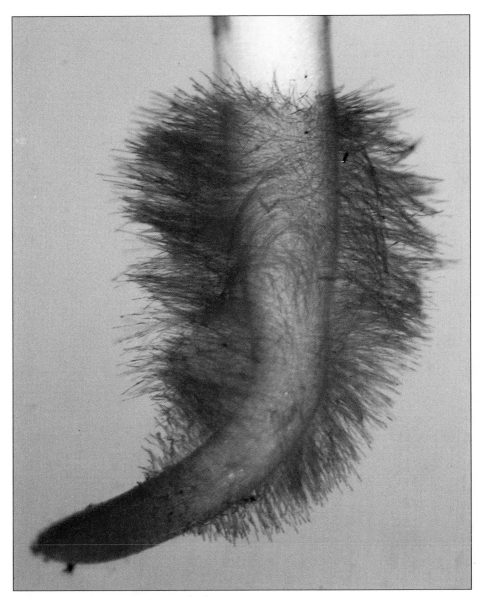

The root hairs on a radish

A shoot (top) and primary root (bottom) are growing out of this corn kernel.

When you plant a seed, a root grows out of the bottom, and a shoot grows out of the top.

The root that grows out of a seed is called the primary root.

Other roots often grow out of the primary root. They are called secondary roots.

This cord grass has many secondary roots.

It's hard to see the difference between the primary root and the secondary roots of this grass.

Sometimes secondary roots are as long and as thick as the primary root.

Some kinds of plants have a very large primary root called a taproot.

The taproot of a dandelion can be several feet long.

A dandelion has a long taproot.

20

Taproots that you can
eat are called root crops.

A carrot is a root crop.
Sweet potatoes, beets,
and radishes are root
crops, too.

Have you ever heard of an air plant?

Their roots grow in the open air instead of under the ground.

Some orchids are air plants.

These orchids are air plants.

Mangrove trees

The roots of a mangrove tree grow from its branches, not its trunk.

These trees grow in shallow water. Often, you can see their roots above the waterline.

A banyan tree also grows
with its roots above
the ground.

Some of the roots are
thick enough to become
new trunks.

Banyan tree

Some banyan trees have more than 3,000 trunks.

That's really putting down roots!

Words You Know

banyan tree

air plant

mangrove tree

primary root

taproot

secondary roots

31

Index

About the Author

Allan Fowler is a freelance writer with a background in advertising.
Born in New York, he now lives in Chicago and enjoys traveling.

Photo Credits